absolute beginners

BODHRÁN
TUTOR

by Conor Long

Transcriptions and Engraving • Gregory Magee
Cover Design • Temple of Design
The Publishers wish to thank Bord Fáilte
for the use of photographs
Editor • Pat Conway

Order No. WM 1405, Cassette: WM 1405T
ISBN No. 1-857200802

Exclusive Distributors:
Walton Manufacturing Co. Ltd.,
2-5 Nth Frederick Street, Dublin 1, Ireland.

Walton Music Inc.,
P.O. Box 874, New York, NY 10009, U.S.A.

Contents

Introduction

"The rattling banjo, old rosin stained fiddles and chirping tin whistles all dance together to the beating rhythm of this round goatskin drum"

Despite occupying a pivotal position in the development of Irish traditional music over the centuries, the bodhrán has only recently attained its deserved status as a "proper" traditional instrument. For many years, it was considered the easy option for those too lazy to learn a real instrument. Today, however, due mostly to the efforts of a handful of excellent players, the bodhrán is accepted as a complex and expressive instrument capable of producing a huge array of dynamic accompaniments from driving contemporary rhythms to the most subtle percussive nuances.

The Book
This book aims to teach the complete beginner the basics of good bodhrán playing with full participation in a traditional session as its principal goal.

The Cassette
The cassette which is available to accompany this book features all the exercises and solos in this tutor.

The Bodhrán – An Irish Frame Drum

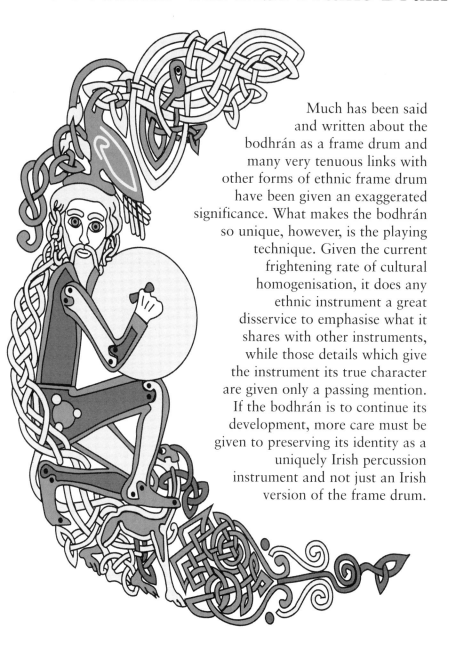

Much has been said and written about the bodhrán as a frame drum and many very tenuous links with other forms of ethnic frame drum have been given an exaggerated significance. What makes the bodhrán so unique, however, is the playing technique. Given the current frightening rate of cultural homogenisation, it does any ethnic instrument a great disservice to emphasise what it shares with other instruments, while those details which give the instrument its true character are given only a passing mention. If the bodhrán is to continue its development, more care must be given to preserving its identity as a uniquely Irish percussion instrument and not just an Irish version of the frame drum.

Choosing a Bodhrán

Today there are a bewildering variety of bodhráns available, from budget priced instrument manufactured in the Far East to custom-made instruments, tuneable and even electric bodhráns. Your choice of instrument should reflect your level of interest and commitment. Don't buy an expensive instrument if you're just getting started. By the time your playing has evolved to a point where you can justify owning a high quality instrument, your idea of what makes a good bodhrán will have altered greatly from when you first started learning.

Here's a short checklist of things to check for when buying your first bodhrán.

THE SIZE
18 inches is most desirable for a beginner; steer clear of smaller sizes. They might look nice on the wall but are difficult to play and don't have much tonal depth.

THE SKIN
Make goatskin your number one choice. It's thicker and less sensitive to changes in room temperature than calfskin. Deer, dog and ginnet skins are also found on non-commercially produced bodhráns. Hold the skin up to the light and check for any small pinholes.

THE RIM
Happily, most of the bodhráns available today use a laminated wooden frame which is stronger and more likely to keep its shape than a more traditional one-piece frame. Avoid anything shallower than 3.5cm (1.5 inches)

THE CROSS-BARS

All bodhráns used to have a full cross to help them keep their shape. However, recent advances in design have meant that this is no longer necessary and the bars are now only used to give the players greater control over skin-dampening and playing position.

THE STICK OR CIPÍN

Personal preference is the key here. Try a selection and take the stick you find most comfortable As your style develops, so too your taste in sticks may change, so keep experimenting all the time.

Bodhrán Care

Bodhráns are definitely a low maintenance instrument. All that's needed is a little care to keep the skin supple and correctly tensioned. Always keep your bodhrán in a cool, dry place, otherwise the skin tension will be too high or too low to allow for decent playing. If at a session you have to wet the skin to reduce tension, use water, not beer! Saddle soap or dubbin can also be used to keep the skin supple and is strongly recommended if you are living in a warm climate.

Playing Styles

Today there are three distinct regional styles of bodhrán playing.

THE HAND STYLE
Simple, but very effective for accompanying songs and slower instrumentals. The principal drawback of this style is its inability to allow for any form of complex or dynamic accompaniment on faster tunes.

THE SINGLE-ENDED STICK or LIMERICK STYLE
This style is more common among older players and is considered by many to be a dying style in a tradition which sets a premium on flowing and subtle accompaniments.

THE DOUBLE-ENDED STICK OR KERRY STYLE
By far the most commonly found and accepted style. The major advantage of this style is in the ease with which it allows the player to produce complex and constantly varying accompaniments to the faster traditional tunes such as jigs, reels, polkas and hornpipes.

This book concentrates on the double-ended stick style. Once you've mastered that, you'll find the other other styles easy enough to assimilate, should the situation call for something different.

Holding the Bodhrán

Place the bodhrán on your left thigh, your hand between the uppermost quarter of the cross-piece and the skin with the side of your thumb (from the knuckle down) placed gently against the skin.

Relax your shoulders and arms and remember that the secret of good fluid playing lies in supple and controlled wrist action, not flailing arms and twitching shoulders.

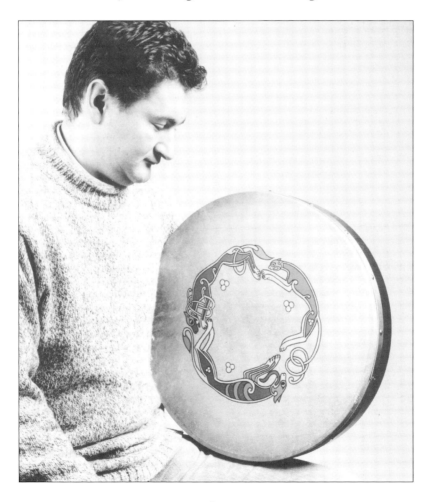

Holding the Stick

Firstly, let's define the stick to avoid any confusion later. The bottom of the stick is the end held closest to your chest, the top of the stick is the end closer to the centre of the bodhrán.

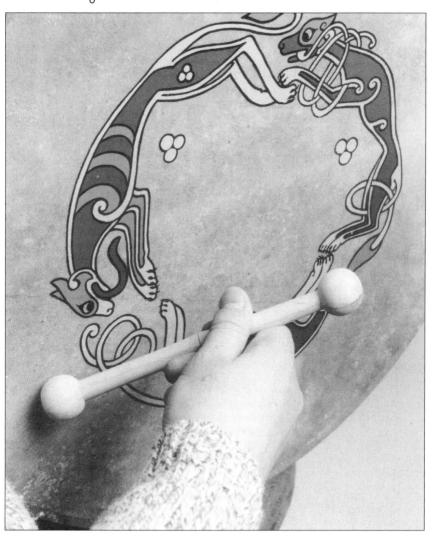

Pick up the stick and hold it as if it were a pen. Now move the stick until your thumb is at a right angle to the stick when held at the centre. You should be holding the stick at an angle roughly parallel to the head with the bottom of the beater next to the skin and the top approximately 3 cm from the skin. Don't grip the stick too tightly – you must allow it a certain degree of freedom to pivot between your thumb and index finger. Given the correct amount of freedom, the bodhrán stick will take on a kind of life of its own which makes smooth, fluid playing a lot easier.

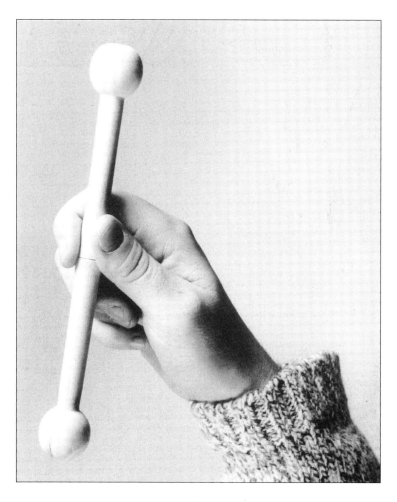

Playing Position

Most of your playing will be done in the third quarter of the skin (clockwise). Downbeats will start at the top of the quarter (9 o'clock) and follow through to just above the bottom of the quarter (7 o'clock). Upbeats are the exact opposite, starting at 7 o'clock and following through to 9 o'clock.

Remember to use only the bottom end of the stick. Good solid rhythms can be achieved using only one end of the stick; as your playing develops, the top of the stick will come into play naturally and without any conscious effort on your behalf.

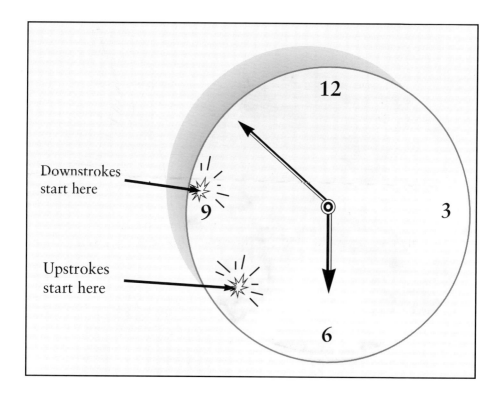

How to Read
Bodhrán Tablature

The idea of music tablature has been around now for some time, being most commonly found in guitar music, where standard music notation fails to provide a sufficiently informative, intuitive and easy-to-grasp method of transcription for those with little or no formal music training.

The bodhrán tablature used in this book has evolved through many years of playing, teaching and selling bodhráns and has been heavily influenced by the comments of pupils, customers and fellow musicians. The following symbols denote the time values for each time you hit the bodhrán.

Symbol	Beat Value	Note Value
●	1 beat	1/4 note
◐	1/2 beat	1/8 note
◑	1/4 beat	1/16 note

When notes are joined together, this means only one hit on the skin but the time value of both notes.

Triplets or double-strokes played with the top of the stick are denoted by a beat symbol resting between the downstroke and upstroke lines and shown below.

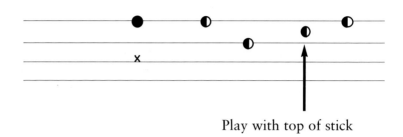

Play with top of stick

Accents

Accents and skin damping are shown using the following symbols:

x Accent or emphasis

∇ Hand on skin

∆ Hand off skin

These values are arranged on a 4-line stave to allow for downstrokes, upstrokes, accents and damping as follows:

Downstrokes
Upstrokes
Accents
Skin Dampen

Let's see how tab can be used to notate a 4/4 pattern of 16th notes. This should give you a clear idea of how tab works.

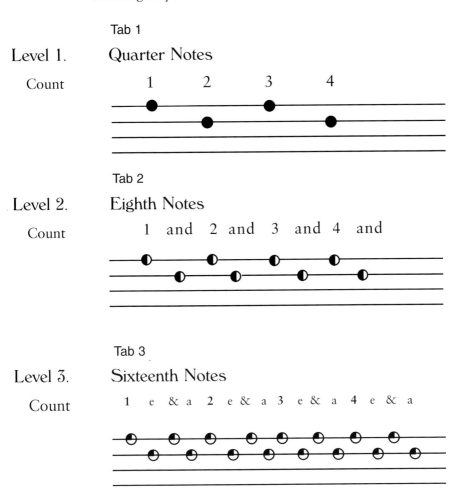

Tab 1

Level 1.   Quarter Notes

Count   1   2   3   4

Tab 2

Level 2.   Eighth Notes

Count   1   and   2   and   3   and   4   and

Tab 3

Level 3.   Sixteenth Notes

Count   1   e   &   a   2   e   &   a   3   e   &   a   4   e   &   a

If you have the recording that accompanies this book you can listen to the examples of each level and count along to see how the notation links to the music. Don't try playing yet; this exercise is intended as an aid to understanding bodhrán tab and not as a playing exercise. Once you have a clear understanding of how this works, you are ready to move on and try some patterns.

Reels (Primary Level)

The reel is by far the most commonly found form of tune played at sessions these days. So if you can master this, you're well on your way. Reels are always played in a 4/4 time signature or, in simple terms, four beats to each bar.

Listening to exercise 1 on the tape, you'll hear a basic 4/4 pattern. Now try playing along using the pattern below.

EX. 1

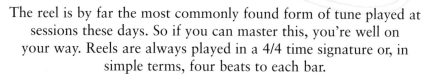

Now let's try adding an extra beat by splitting the third beat into two half beats. Listen to exercise 2 on the tape, then try it with the pattern below.

EX. 2

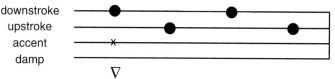

If we put both of these patterns together, we'll get a two bar pattern sufficiently complex to accompany a basic slow reel. Note the shift of accent on the second beat. If you have the cassette, try playing along to the tune

EX. 3

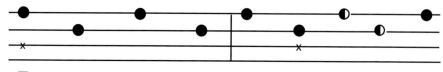

Jigs (Primary Level)

Although regarded by many as the poor relative of the reel, the jig still remains a very popular form of tune at sessions, particularly where musicians are more relaxed and less competitive about their playing. From the bodhrán player's point of view, it provides an opportunity for very open and relaxed playing with plenty of scope for swinging the rhythm with the mood of the other players.

The jig is in 6/8 time, or six half beats to the bar.
Listen to exercise 4 on the tape, then try the pattern as follows.

EX. 4

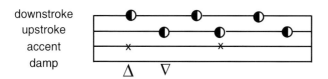

Note the relaxing of the hand to skin tension on the first beat of each bar, following with another accent on beat 4.

Dropping the second beat from this pattern will give extra emphasis to the beginning of each and give the melody a bit more rhythmic space. Again, if you have the recording, listen to Ex. 5. Once you are comfortable with it. You can use this pattern for simple jigs. Make sure to emphasise the 4th beat on the upstroke.

EX. 5

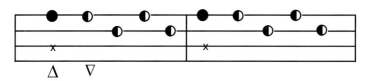

If you have the cassette, try playing along to the tune.

Reels (Secondary Level)

Now that you've gotten the hang of the two principal rhythms used in Irish music, let's try building a more complex reel accompaniment using shifting accents. Before starting this section, take a few minutes to run through the patterns you learned in the primary level reel section.

Now listen to exercise 6 on the recording a few times. Then try playing along as below:

EX. 6

downstroke
upstroke
accent
damp

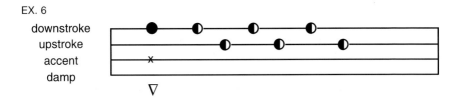

Let's try that over four bars with some variation:

EX. 7

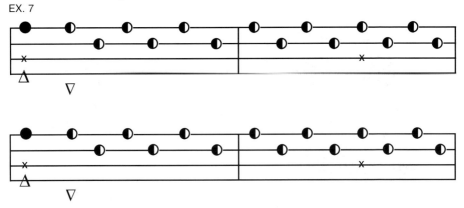

With this pattern under your belt you should now be able to play a more complex reel accompaniment. If you have the cassette, try playing along to exercise 8

THE MOST COMMON WAYS OF VARYING A TUNE ARE AS FOLLOWS:

• Shifting around accents within the tune.

• Skipping particular beats to add more space to the rhythm.
  (This is especially effective on upstrokes.)

• Changing the pitch of the skin by varying skin tension
  with your left hand.

• Using the rim of the bodhrán to produce a harder, more raspy
  accent than produced by the skin.

• Moving your playing position away from the standard 9-7
  position on certain beats to give more varied tone.

Many of today's great players have their own very individual
techniques. The secret here lies in experimentation and listening
very closely to the playing of your fellow musicians.

Jigs (Secondary Level)

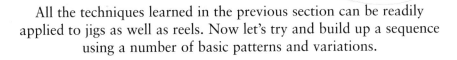

All the techniques learned in the previous section can be readily applied to jigs as well as reels. Now let's try and build up a sequence using a number of basic patterns and variations.

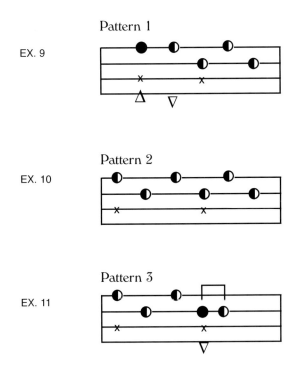

By combining these three patterns in various orders and applying the accents along with damping, we can produce a solid interesting accompaniment.

Here is an example of a four bar sequence using
the previous three patterns:

EX. 12

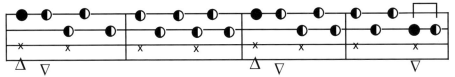

This pattern can be used to provide a more complex and varied sound.
If you have the cassette, try playing along with the tune
Remember, you should be able to play all these patterns using
just the bottom end of the stick. Now let's try introducing the
top end of the stick, putting a triplet into pattern 1.

The accompanying recording to
this book goes as follows:

EX. 13

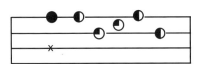

Notice the extra beat using the top end of the stick between
beats 4 and 5. This is called a triplet. To achieve this, tighten the
angle of the stick relative to the bodhrán. Try to loosen your grip
on it as much as possible. With some practice, you'll be able to
drop in triplets with ease anywhere in the tune without
losing track of the basic rhythm.

Other Forms of Tunes

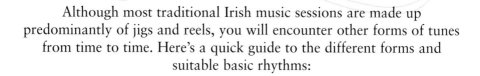

Although most traditional Irish music sessions are made up
predominantly of jigs and reels, you will encounter other forms of tunes
from time to time. Here's a quick guide to the different forms and
suitable basic rhythms:

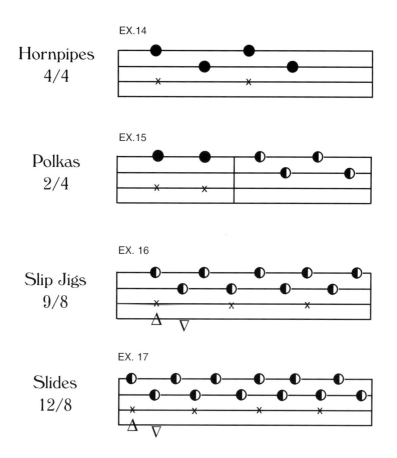

All these types of tunes require a large amount of 'following the tune' and
are therefore best left until your playing of jigs and reels is better
developed and your session ear more finely tuned.

Session Playing

When playing at a session, follow a few simple rules and you'll be given a fair chance by other musicians.

1   Always sit in on a session for about fifteen minutes before you start to play. This gives you a chance to "suss out" the hierarchy of the session and the dynamics of the individual players.

2   Never start a tune yourself or batter away needlessly between tunes.

3   If a tune is new to you, play along tapping your stick on the outside of your right thigh. You may not be able to hear it but you'll feel the rhythm enough to get you started without bringing the session to a halt.

4   If in doubt, don't play.

5   Once you're up and running, don't forget that your playing is providing the heartbeat of the session. If you go wrong, there's a good chance that you'll confuse the other musicians as well. The best rule here is 'don't move from the groove.'

6   Don't overuse a particular technique you may have developed. What's seldom is wonderful.

Here are some tunes for you to play

The Swallow's Tail

EX. 18   Jig 1   Jig 2   Jig

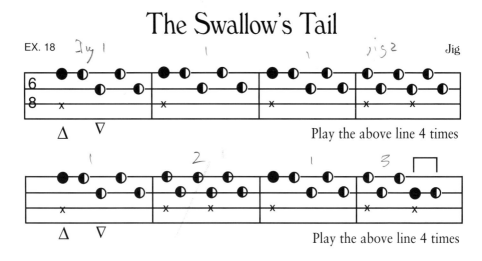

Play the above line 4 times

Play the above line 4 times

The Tenpenny Bit

EX. 19   Jig

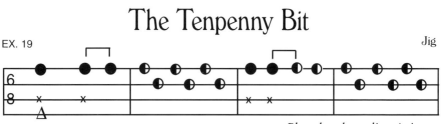

Play the above line 4 times

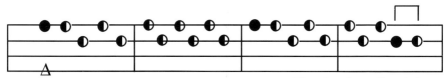

Play the above line 4 times

The Dingle Regatta

Jig

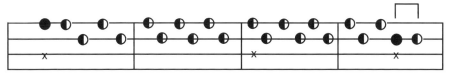

Play the above two lines 6 times

A Fig For a Kiss

Slip Jig

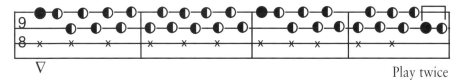

Play twice

Play twice

The Sailor's Bonnet

Reel

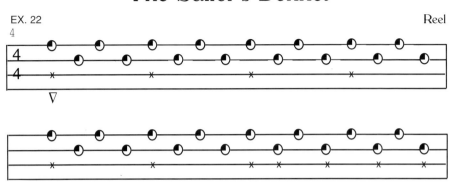

The Dunmore Lasses

Reel

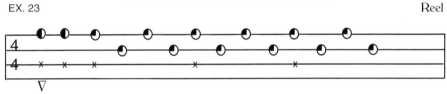

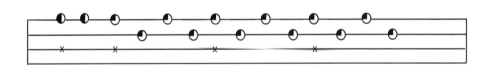

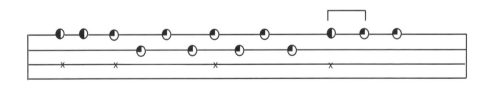

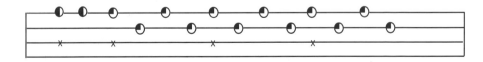

The Harvest Home

Hornpipe

The Ballydesmond Polka

Polka

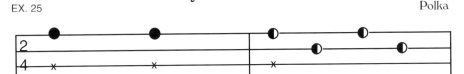

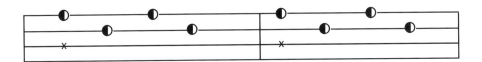

The Nine Points of Roguery

Reel

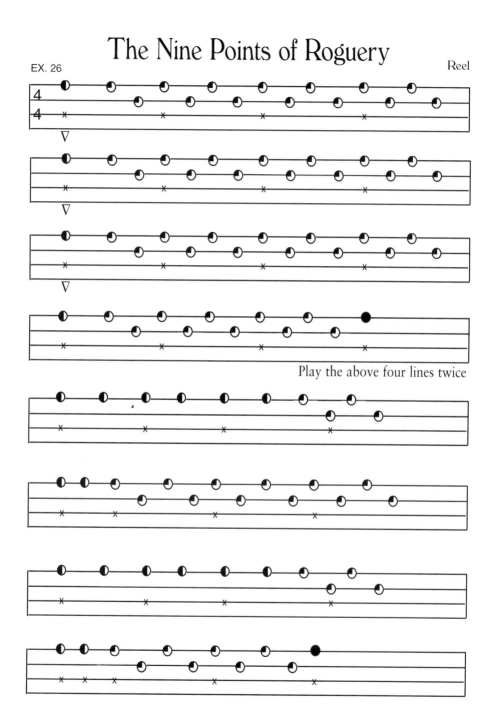

Play the above four lines twice

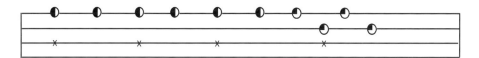

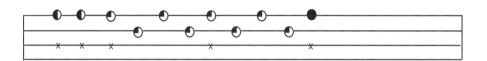

Recommended Listening

It is often said that the best bodhrán players are also great listeners – and it could well be true. So, if you're new to Irish music, make sure you listen to plenty of good traditional music, either live or recorded. Don't limit yourself to recordings that include bodhrán, as bodhrán-free albums are better to practise to and help you to develop your own individual style. Here's a selection of albums well worth checking out.

Where bodhrán is featured, the name of the player is given in brackets after the album title.

1. Arcady (Ringo McDonagh)
2. The Bothy Band (Donal Lunny)
3. Donal Lunny Band (Damien Quinn)
4. Tommy Hayes *An Rás* (Tommy Hayes)
5. Mary Bergin *Feadóga Stáin* (Ringo McDonagh
6. Mícheál Ó Súilleabháin *The Dolphin's Way* (Colm Murphy)
7. Elixir (Hopi Hopkins)
8. The Chieftains *Live* (Kevin Conneff)
9. Planxty (Christy Moore)
10. Matt Molloy *The Heathery Breeze*
11. Seán Smyth *The Blue Fiddle*
12. Frankie Gavin *Irlande*
13. Matt Molloy, Paul Brady, Tommy Peoples
14. Four Men and a Dog *Shifting Gravel* (Gino Lupari)
15. Arty McGlynn & Nollaig Casey *Lead the Knave* (Christy Moore).
16. Colm Murphy *The Bodhrán*
17. Ivan Smyth *Bodhrán Champion of Ireland*
18. Dervish *Live in Palma* (Cathy Jordan)
19. Nomos *Set You Free* (Frank Torpey)
20. Kila *Tóg é Go Bog é*.

The accompanying recording contains a selection of tunes for you to play along with.

absolute beginners *video*

A fabulous 40-minute teaching video for beginners.

An easy to use video for anyone taking up the bodhrán for the first time and who wants to start playing immediately.

Learn to play your first basic strokes and accompany tunes ... it's very easy.

absolute
BEGINNERS   Conor Long

Guide to Playing the

BODHRÁN

A fabulous teaching video for beginners.
Learn to play your first basic strokes and
accompany tunes. It's very easy!

COMPLETE WITH LIVE STAGE PERFORMANCES FEATURING...
GAVIN RALSTON - GUITAR · PAUL McNEVIN - FIDDLE

Complete with live stage performances featuring Gerry O'Connor - banjo and Paul McNevin - fiddle.